# Letterland

## Contents

# Level 2 - Student Book 1

Clever Cat and Harry Hat Man make a different sound when they are together. Listen.

I'm Clever Cat. I say 'c'.

I'm Harry Hat Man. I say 'hhh'.

## Two letters together!

When Clever Cat is next to Harry, his hairy hat makes her sneeze, 'ch!'.

**Letter sounds** Use your *Picture Code Cards* to review Clever Cat and Harry Hat Man's sound. Then look at the new sound they make when they are together.

Code Card

Listen to the story about what happens when Clever Cat and Harry Hat Man come together in a word.

# Clever Cat and Harry Hat Man

**ch digraph** Listen again to the story. This time look for the things in the picture that have the 'ch' sound.

Find these items in the picture. Listen for the 'ch' sound at the start or middle of the words.

chin

chair

chicken

peaches

children

### Phonics Online

Listen to the story about Clever Cat and Harry Hat Man.
Sing along to the song, listen to the sound and play the games.

Letterland
**Phonics Online**

Workbook

When you have finished this page, complete the **ch** activities in *Workbook 1*, pages 2-4.

Workbook

Build some **ch** words using *Phonics Online* or the *Picture Code Cards*.

Code Card

## Build it!

chin, chop, chick, lunch, munch.

**Let's read!** ➤

Use the Sound Slide trick to blend the sounds together and read the words. Then try reading the sentences with more fluency.

It is lunch. Munch, munch, munch!

He can chop logs.

Song 🎵🎵

Listen to Clever Cat and Harry Hat Man's song. If you can, join in with the chorus when you listen for the second time.

Track 05

I'm Sammy Snake. I say, 'sss'.

I'm Harry Hat Man. I say, 'hhh'.

## Two letters together!

Harry Hat Man hates noise so when Sammy Snake sits behind him, hissing 'sss', Harry turns to him and says, 'sh!'.

**Letter sounds** Use your *Picture Code Cards* to review Sammy Snake and Harry Hat Man's sound. Then look at the new sound they make when they are together.

Listen to the story about what happens when Sammy Snake and Harry Hat Man come together in a word.

# Sammy Snake and Harry Hat Man

**sh digraph** Listen again to the story. This time look for the things in the picture that have the '**sh**' sound.

7

Find these items in the picture. Listen for the 'sh' sound at the start or the end of the words.

Track 08

## shop

## ship

## shell

## fish

## shoe

**Phonics Online**

Listen to the story about Sammy Snake and Harry Hat Man.
Sing along to the song, listen to the sound and play the games.

Workbook

When you have finished this page, complete the **sh** activities in Workbook 1, pages 5-7.

Workbook

Build some **sh** words using *Phonics Online* or the *Picture Code Cards*.

## Build it!

ship, shop, shell, fish, shed.

**Let's read!**

Use the Sound Slide trick to blend the sounds together and read the words. Then try reading the sentences with more fluency.

## She sells shells on a ship.

Sea shells

## He sells fish in a shop.

Fresh Fish

Song ♪♫♪ Listen to Sammy Snake and Harry Hat Man's song. If you can, join in with the chorus when you listen for the second time.

Track 09

Talking Tess and Harry Hat Man make a different sound when they are together. Listen.

Track 10

I'm Talking Tess. I say, 't'.

I'm Harry Hat Man. I say, 'hhh'.

## Two letters together!

Harry and Tess both think that the thunder is too loud.

th!

**Letter sounds** Use your *Picture Code Cards* to review Talking Tess and Harry Hat Man's sound. Then look at the new sound they make when they are together.

 **Explore**

Listen to the story of what happens when Talking Tess and Harry Hat Man come together in a word.

Track 11

# Talking Tess and Harry Hat Man

th digraph
Listen again to the story. This time look for the things in the picture that have the '**th**' sound.

Find these items in the picture. Listen for the '**th**' sound at the start or the end of the words.

Track 12

**throw**

thank you

**thank you**

3

**three**

**bath**

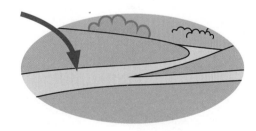

**path**

### Phonics Online

Listen to the story about Talking Tess and Harry Hat Man.
Sing along to the song, listen to the sound and play the games.

Workbook

When you have finished this page, complete the **th** activities in *Workbook 1*, pages 8-10.

Workbook

Build some **th** words using *Phonics Online* or the *Picture Code Cards*.

## Build it!

think, thin,
cloth, bath.

**Let's read!** ➤  Use the Sound Slide trick to blend the sounds together and read the words. Then try reading the sentences with more fluency.

# I think she is thin.

# He thinks so much!

**Song** 🎵 Listen to Talking Tess and Harry Hat Man's song. If you can, join in with the chorus when you listen for the second time.

Track 13

**Sound** ▶ Talking Tess and Harry Hat Man make two different sounds when they come together. Listen.

Track 14

th**under**

the th**under**

## Tricky words

this hat

that hat

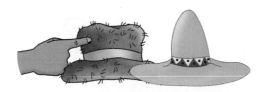

these hats

those hats

Workbook

The first '**th**' sound is unvoiced or whispered, as in th̲ink. The second '**th**' sound is voiced, as in **th**at. Now complete page 11 of *Workbook 1*.

**Story** ➤ Let's see what happens when Walter Walrus sits next to Harry Hat Man in a word.

Track 15

# Walter Walrus's water tricks!

Watch out when Walter Walrus is about!

Walter Walrus hates it when Harry Hat Man stands ahead of him. He's so tall and he wears a hat! So what does Walter do? He splashes Harry's hat off! Harry is too surprised to speak, so you will just hear Walter saying 'w!'

**Note** ➤ In a few words, Harry gets annoyed at Walter. He grabs a bucket of water and throws it over Walter, saying, "**Wh**o do you think you are?" Then you will just hear Harry's '**h**...' sound.

**Letter sounds** Use your *Picture Code Cards* to review Walter Walrus and Harry Hat Man's sound. Then look at the new sound they make when they are together.

Code Card

15

Listen to the story about Walter Walrus splashing Harry Hat Man with salty water.

Track 16

WHITLEY BAY

WHEAT GERM

# Walter Walrus and Harry Hat Man

wh digraph

Listen again to the story. This time look for the things in the picture where you can hear Walter.

Find these items in the picture. Listen for Walter saying '**w**!' and Harry staying quiet in these words.

## wheel

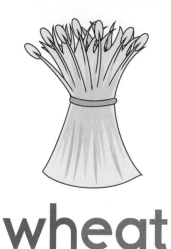

## wheat

## whale

## white

## whistle

### Phonics Online

Listen to the story about Walter Walrus and Harry Hat Man. Sing along to the song, listen to the sound and play the games.

Workbook

When you have finished this page, complete the **wh** activities in *Workbook 1*, pages 12-13.

Workbook

Build some **wh** words using *Phonics Online* or the *Picture Code Cards*.

Code Card

## Build it!

when, which, whisk.

**Let's read!** ▶

Use the Sound Slide trick to blend the sounds together and read the words. Then try reading the sentences with more fluency.

When will he get up?

Which hat is his?

Song

Listen to Walter Walrus and Harry Hat Man's song. If you can, join in with the chorus when you listen for the second time.

Track 18

## Peter Puppy and Harry Hat Man!

Peter Puppy loves having his photograph taken. So whenever Harry Hat Man is next to him in a word, he turns and takes his photo.

Peter Puppy smiles and Harry laughs, quietly though, with his teeth on his lips. So his usual 'hhh...' sound becomes a 'fff...' sound.

## Listen and click!

Track 20 — Listen and pretend to take a photo if you hear the '**ph**' sound in these words.

hand    tree    house    phone

photo    elephant    card    dolphin    trophy

**Letter sounds** Use your *Picture Code Cards* to review Peter Puppy and Harry Hat Man's sound. Then look at the new sound they make when they are together.

Code Card

Listen to the story about Harry taking Peter Puppy's photograph.

# Peter Puppy and Harry Hat Man

 ph digraph

Listen again to the story. This time look for the things in the picture where you can hear Harry laughing.

Find these items in the picture. Listen out for Harry quietly laughing in them.

elephant

telephone

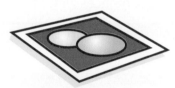

photograph

alphabet

dolphin

## Phonics Online

Listen to the story about Peter Puppy and Harry Hat Man. Sing along to the song, listen to the sound and play the games.

Workbook

When you have finished this page, complete the **ph** activities in *Workbook 1*, pages 15-17.

Workbook

Build some **ph** words using *Phonics Online* or the *Picture Code Cards*.

Code Card

## Build it!   photo, dolphin, alphabet, graph.

**Let's read!**

Use the Sound Slide trick to blend the sounds together and read the words. Then try reading the sentences with more fluency.

# The dolphin can swim.

# The elephant has thick legs.

 ♫♪ Song   Listen to Peter Puppy and Harry Hat Man's song. If you can, join in with the chorus when you listen for the second time.

 Track 23

Read the stories in *Phonics Readers 1*, featuring the phonic elements in this Unit.

# Comprehension  Point to the correct answer.

1. What did Firefighter Fred pick up?

○ hens            ☐ chicks

2. What did Firefighter Fred do next?

○ chop logs            ☐ chop chips

3. Where did he get Shep?

○ in a shop            ☐ on a ship

4. Where does Shep nap?

○ on a ship            ☐ in a shed

5. What thing has a fin in this story?

○ a dolphin            ☐ a duck

**Pair work**

When you have read the stories, the teacher will read the questions. Work in pairs or small groups to read and point to the correct answers.

**Stickers** → Complete the sticker activity in *Workbook 1*, pages 18-19.

**Listen** → Complete the exercises in *Workbook 1*, pages 20-21.

**Talk time** → Review some language introduced in Level 1. Work in pairs asking the questions and choosing answers, then swap.

Track 26

**What shape is it?**
It is a ...

circle    triangle    square

**What colour is it?**
It is ...

yellow        orange        white        black

green         red           pink         blue

**How old are you?**
I am _ years old.

1 2 3 4 5 6 7 8 9 10
one two three four five six seven eight nine ten

**What day is it?**
It is ...

Monday   Tuesday   Wednesday   Thursday   Friday
Saturday   Sunday  - the weekend

**What can you do?**
I can...

count       smile       wave       point       sit down

**Where is it?**
It is ...

under          in          on

**Pair work** — It is a good idea to come back to these questions over and over again to improve fluency.

This is Mr E's Magic **e**. The Silent Magic **e** shoots sparks over one letter to make a Vowel Man appear.

### Silent Magic e!

This **e** you cannot hear.
It can make a Vowel
Man appear.

hat → hate

cap → cape

**Letter sounds** Show the *Picture Code Card* and do the action of waving like the vowel man as you say his name.

25

 **Explore**

Listen to the story about how Silent Magic **e** makes Mr A appear.

Track 28

# Magic e makes Mr A appear

 a_e split digraph

Listen again to the story. This time look for the things in the picture in which Mr A has appeared to say his name.

Find these items in the picture. Listen for Mr A saying his name in the words.

## gate

## cake

## grapes

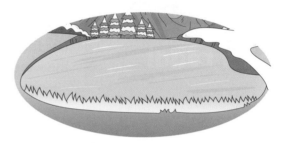

## lake

## skate

### Phonics Online

Listen to the story about Silent Magic **e** making Mr A appear. Sing along to the song, listen to the sound and play the games.

Workbook — When you have finished this page, complete the a_e activities in *Workbook 1*, pages 22-24.

**27**

**Word Building** ➤

Build some **a_e** words using *Phonics Online* or the *Picture Code Cards*.

## Build it! plane, plate, cake, lake, gate, skate.

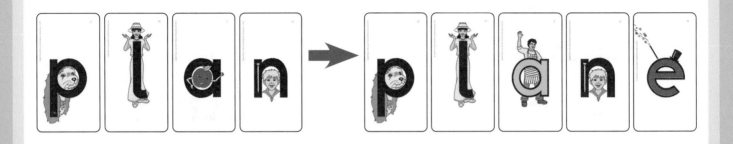

**Let's read!** ➤

Use the Sound Slide trick to blend the sounds together and read the words. Then try reading the sentences with more fluency.

Nick has a cake and grapes.

She can skate on a lake!

 Song 🎵 Listen to the Magic **e** song. If you can, join in with the chorus when you listen for the second time.

Track 31

Good day, I'm Mr A.
I say my name, 'a'.

Hi. I'm Mr I.
I say my name, 'i'.

# When we go out walking...

a...

When two vowels go out walking, the first one does the talking.

The first one says his name, 'a', but his friend won't do the same.

**Letter sounds** The first Vowel Man says his name. The second Vowel Man stays quiet. He's too busy looking out for robots.

Listen to the story about Mr A and Mr I out walking in words.

# Mr A and Mr I out walking

ai digraph

Listen again to the story. This time look for the things in the picture in which Mr A and Mr I are out walking in the word.

**Keywords**

Find these items in the picture. Listen for Mr A saying his name in the words.

Track 33

# rain

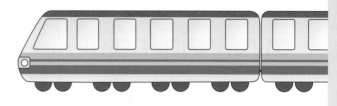

# train

# snail

# chain

# paint

## Phonics Online

Listen to the story about Mr A and Mr I out walking.
Sing along to the song, listen to the sound and play the games.

Letterland
**Phonics Online**

Workbook

When you have finished this page, complete the **ai** activities in *Workbook 1*, pages 25-27.

Workbook

31

Build some **ai** words using *Phonics Online* or the *Picture Code Cards.*

# Build it!

rain, train, paint
sail, nail, snail.

**Let's read!**

Use the Sound Slide trick to blend the sounds together and read the words. Then try reading the sentences with more fluency.

## The snail is on a train.

## It's raining on the sails.

Song

Listen to the Vowels Out Walking song. If you can, join in with the chorus when you listen for the second time.

Track 34

Track 35

Good day, I'm Mr A.
I say my name, 'a'.

I'm Yellow Yo-yo Man.
I say, 'y'.

# When we go out walking...

a...

When these two go out walking, Mr A does the talking.

Mr A says his name, 'a', but his friend won't do the same.

**Letter sounds** Mr I gets dizzy at the **end** of words. So then Mr A goes out walking with Yellow Yo-yo Man instead.

**Explore**

Listen to the story about Mr A and Yellow Yo-yo Man out walking in words. Today they are going on holiday.

Track 36

# Mr A and Yellow Yo-yo Man

ay digraph

Listen again to the story. This time look for the things in the picture in which Mr A and Yellow Yo-yo Man are out walking in the word.

Find these items in the picture. Listen for Mr A saying his name in the words.

Track 37

## spray

## takeaway

Holiday getaway

Letterland Bay

## holiday

Word Play

X-RAY TRAY

## tray

## play

### Phonics Online

Listen to the story about Mr A and Yellow Yo-yo Man out walking. Sing along to the song, listen to the sound and play the games.

LetterLand Phonics Online

Workbook

When you have finished this page, complete the **ay** activities in *Workbook 1*, pages 28-30.

Workbook

**35**

Build some **ay** words using *Phonics Online* or the *Picture Code Cards*.

## Build it!

day, hay, pay, say,
way, tray, play, spray.

**Let's read!**

Use the Sound Slide trick to blend the sounds together and read the words. Then try reading the sentences with more fluency.

Tess has a takeaway on a tray.

Today is Sunday, the 4th of May.

**Song** Listen to the Vowels Out Walking Song. This is the same song as you heard for Mr A and Mr I out walking. Try to join in this time!

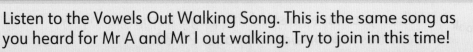

Read the stories in *Phonics Readers 2*, featuring the phonic elements in this Unit.

# Comprehension

Point to the correct answer.

1. What are the Letterland friends looking for?

◯ a safe plan ☐ a safe place

2. What is the name of Kate's dog?

◯ Kane ☐ Kate

3. What does Kate put on top of the cake?

◯ eggs ☐ grapes

4. What does Kane yap at? Point to **two** correct answers.

◯ the train ☐ his tail

△ the lake ⬡ the rain

**Pair work**

When you have read the stories, the teacher will read the questions. Work in pairs or small groups to read and point to the correct answers.

**Stickers** ➡ Complete the sticker activity in *Workbook 1*, pages 32-33.

**Listen** ➡ Complete the exercises in *Workbook 1*, pages 34-35.

**Talk time** ➡ Look at the chart below showing the weather forecast for a week. Revise days of the week and describe the weather.

Track 42

| | | |
|---|---|---|
| Monday | | cloudy |
| Tuesday | | rainy |
| Wednesday | | sunny |
| Thursday | | windy |
| Friday | | snowy |
| Saturday | | cloudy |
| Sunday | | sunny |

You try. The weather forecast is in the future.

**On Monday,** it will be **cloudy. On Tuesday,** it will be...

Tenses

Think about the past, present and future tenses of the verb 'to be'. Yesterday it *was* rainy, today it *is* sunny, tomorrow it *will be* windy.

This is Mr E's Magic **e**. The Silent Magic **e** shoots sparks over one letter to make a Vowel Man appear.

## Silent Magic e!

You know this e you cannot hear. It can make a Vowel Man appear.

complete

These magic sparks make me appear and say my name 'e'.

these

**Letter sounds** Look how the magic sparks shoot over one letter to make the Vowel Man appear and say his name.

**Explore** ➔

Listen to the story about Silent Magic **e** making Mr E appear.

# Magic e makes Mr E appear

40

e_e split digraph

Listen again to the story. This time look for the things in the picture in which Mr E has appeared to say his name.

**Keywords** ▶

Find these items in the picture. Listen for Mr E saying his name in the words.

Track
45

# complete

# delete

# scene

# compete

# athlete

## Phonics Online

Listen to the story about Magic **e** making Mr E appear.
Sing along to the song, listen to the sound and play the games.

Workbook

When you have finished this page, complete the e_e activities in *Workbook 1*, pages 36-38.

Workbook

**41**

Build some **e_e** words using *Phonics Online* or the *Picture Code Cards*.

## Build it! athlete, compete, complete.

  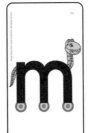    

**Let's read!** ⟩

Use the Sound Slide trick to blend the sounds together and read the words. Then try reading the sentences with more fluency.

The athletes compete to win.

She completes and wins!

 Song

Listen to the Magic **e** song. If you can, join in with the chorus when you listen for the second time.

 Track 46

When Mr E and his brother Mr E are together out walking, you'll only hear the first Mr E talking.

Track 47

Greetings, I'm Mr E.
I say my name, 'e'.

Hi. I'm Mr E's brother.
I also say my name, 'e'.

# When we go out walking...

e...

When two e's go out walking, the first Mr E does the talking.

He just says his name, 'e', but his brother won't do the same.

**Letter sounds** The first Vowel Man says his name. The second Vowel Man stays quiet. He's too busy looking out for robots.

**Explore**

Listen to the story about Mr E and his brother out walking in words.

Track 48

# Mr E and his brother out walking

ee digraph

Listen again to the story. This time look for the things in the picture in which Mr E and his brother are out walking in the word.

Find these items in the picture. Listen for Mr E saying his name in the words.

**tree**

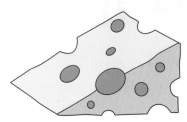

**cheese**

**jeep**

**sleep**

**sweep**

### Phonics Online

Listen to the story about Mr E and his brother out walking. Sing along to the song, listen to the sound and play the games.

Workbook

When you have finished this page, complete the **ee** activities in *Workbook 1*, pages 39-41.

Workbook

45

Build some **ee** words using *Phonics Online*, or the *Picture Code Cards*.

Code Card

## Build it!

jeep, sleep,
sweep,
street, green.

**Let's read!**

Use the Sound Slide trick to blend the sounds together and read the words. Then try reading the sentences with more fluency.

Three bees in green trees.

The man is sweeping the street.

**Song** Listen to the Vowels Out Walking song. If you can, join in with the chorus when you listen for the second time.

Track 50

When Mr E and Mr A are out walking, you'll only hear Mr E talking. Listen to the reason why.

Track 51

Greetings, I'm Mr E.
I say my name, 'e'.

Good day. I'm Mr A.
I say my name, 'a'.

# When we go out walking...

e...

When these two go out walking, Mr E does the talking.

Mr E says his name, 'e', but his friend won't do the same.

**Letter sounds** The first Vowel Man says his name. The second Vowel Man stays quiet. He's too busy looking out for robots.

**Explore** ➡ Listen to the story about Mr E and Mr A out walking in words.

Track 52

# Mr E and Mr A out walking

ea digraph

Listen again to the story. This time look for the things in the picture in which Mr E and Mr A are out walking in the word.

Find these items in the picture. Listen for Mr E saying his name in these words.

Track 53

## peach

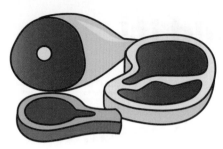

## meat

## peas

## tea

## leaf

### Phonics Online

Listen to the story about Mr E and Mr A out walking.
Sing along to the song, listen to the sound and play the games.

Phonics Online

**Workbook** When you have finished this page, complete the **ea** activities in *Workbook 1*, pages 42-44.

Workbook

49

Build some **ea** words using *Phonics Online*, or the *Picture Code Cards*.

Code Card

## Build it!

tea, eat, pea, peach, beach, meat, leaf.

**Let's read!**

Use the Sound Slide trick to blend the sounds together and read the words. Then try reading the sentences with more fluency.

Cheap deals on peas and beans!

He eats peaches on the beach.

**50**

🎵 Song

Listen to the Vowels Out Walking song. If you can, join in with the chorus when you listen for the second time.

Track 54

Let's see what happens when Yellow Yo-yo Man helps out at the end of words.

I'm Yellow Yo-yo Man.
I say, 'y'.

I help Mr E at the end
of some words.

## Yo-yo Man works for Mr E

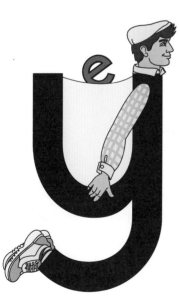

Yellow Yo-yo Man works for Mr E at the end of thousands of words like copy, empty and windy.

**Letter sounds**  At the end of words, a y can sound like an e.

**Explore** ➡ Listen to the story about Yellow Yo-yo Man working for Mr E.

Track
56

# Yellow Yo-yo Man helps Mr E

y as e

Listen to the story and look for the things in which Yellow Yo-yo Man is helping Mr E.

**Keywords**

Find these items in the big picture.
Listen for Yellow Yo-yo Man saying '**e**' for Mr E.

Track
57

# family

# party

# puppy

# teddy

# story

### Phonics Online

Listen to the story about Yellow
Yo-yo Man helping out Mr E.
Sing along to the song, listen to
the sound and play the games.

Workbook

When you have finished this page, complete the y as e
activities in *Workbook 1*, pages 45-47.

Workbook

Build some **y** words using *Phonics Online*, or the *Picture Code Cards*.

Code Card

## Build it!

puppy, teddy, happy, funny, rainy, windy, frosty, mummy, daddy.

**Let's read!**

Use the Sound Slide trick to blend the sounds together and read the words. Then try reading the sentences with more fluency.

It is hot and sunny today.

It is cold and rainy today.

Song

Listen to the chant. If you can, join in when you listen for the second time.

Track 58

Read the stories in *Phonics Readers 3*, featuring the phonic elements in this Unit.

Letterland
Phonics Readers 3
**A trip to the sea**
and other stories

Focus on:
• ee as in sea
• ee as in bee
• y as in baby

Three decodable stories

# Comprehension  Point to the correct answer.

**A trip to the sea**

Focus on: ea as in sea

1. Where were the crabs hiding?

◯ in the rocks  ☐ in the seaweed

2. Who put their hand in the bucket?

◯ Jean  ☐ dad

**Mr E's trees**

Tricky words: here, are

Focus on: ee as in bee

3. Is it free to take sweets from the Sweety Tree?

◯ yes  ☐ no

4. Which tree says, 'yippee!'?

◯ Sleepy Tree  ☐ Squeezy Tree

**Happy!**

Focus on: y as in baby

5. What does the puppy run with?

◯ a bunny  ☐ a pony

**Pair work**  When you have read the stories, the teacher will read the questions. Work in pairs or small groups to read and point to the correct answers.

**Stickers** ➤ Complete the sticker activity in *Workbook 1*, page 49.

**Listen** ➤ Complete the exercises in *Workbook 1*, pages 50-51.

**Talk time** ➤ Describing people. In pairs, each draw two people on a piece of paper. Describe one. Your partner must point to the correct one.

Track 62

## What does he look like?   or   What does she look like?

He is tall.

He is short.

She has long hair.

She has short hair.

She has blue eyes.

She has straight hair.

He has curly hair.

He is bald.

She wears glasses.

He has green eyes.

**Pair work** — Simple stick people drawings are fine. You can draw funny-looking people too, or just describe people in your class.

This is Mr E's Magic **e**. The Silent Magic e shoots sparks over one letter to make a Vowel Man appear.

## Silent Magic e!

You know this e you cannot hear.

It can make a Vowel Man appear.

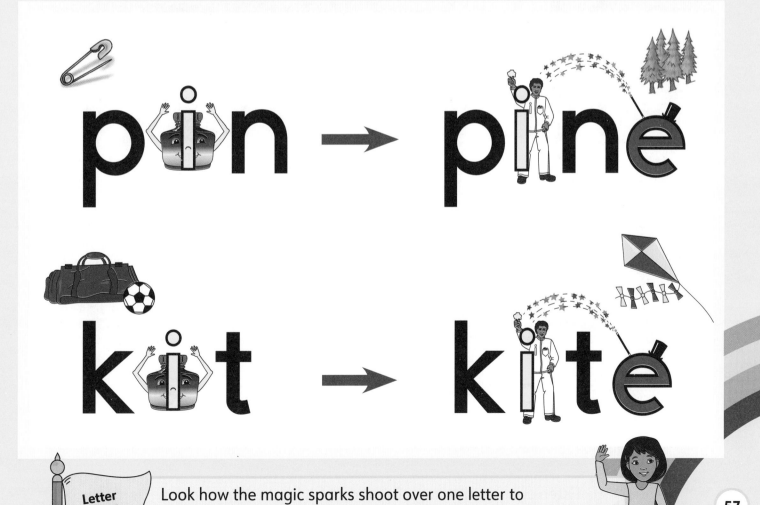

pin → pine

kit → kite

Look how the magic sparks shoot over one letter to make the Vowel Man appear and say his name.

 **Explore**

Listen to the story about how Silent Magic **e** makes Mr I appear.

Track 64

# Magic e makes Mr I appear

i_e split digraph

Listen again to the story. This time look for the things in the picture in which Mr I has appeared to say his name.

Find these items in the picture. Listen for Mr I saying his name in the words.

 Track 65

slide

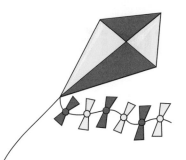

kite

bike

lime

mice

## Phonics Online

Listen to the story about Magic **e** making Mr I appear. Sing along to the song, listen to the sound and play the games.

**Note** NOTE: Sometimes a 'c' can sound like 's'. You will hear this in words like: ra**c**e, pla**c**e, i**c**e, mi**c**e and ni**c**e. You will learn more about this in Level 3.

 Workbook When you have finished this page, complete the i_e activities in *Workbook 1*, pages 52-54.  Workbook

Build some **i_e** words using *Phonics Online*, or the *Picture Code Cards*.

## Build it! kite, bite, bike, slide, hide.

**Let's read!**

Use the Sound Slide trick to blend the sounds together and read the words. Then try reading the sentences with more fluency.

# She likes to ride a bike.

# I like lime and ice.

Song

Listen to the Magic **e** song. If you can, join in with the chorus when you listen for the second time.

Track 66

When Mr I and Mr E are out walking together, you'll usually hear Mr I saying his name. Listen to the reason why.

Hi, I'm Mr I. You know I like to say my name, 'i'.

Greetings. I'm Mr E. I say my name, 'e', in words.

# When we go out walking...

i...

When two vowels go out walking, Mr I usually does the talking.

He just says his name, 'i', but his friend won't do the same.

**Letter sounds** The first Vowel Man says his name. The second Vowel Man stays quiet. He's too busy looking out for robots.

 **Explore** Look at the picture of Mr I and Mr E out walking.
Can you find the Keywords in the picture?

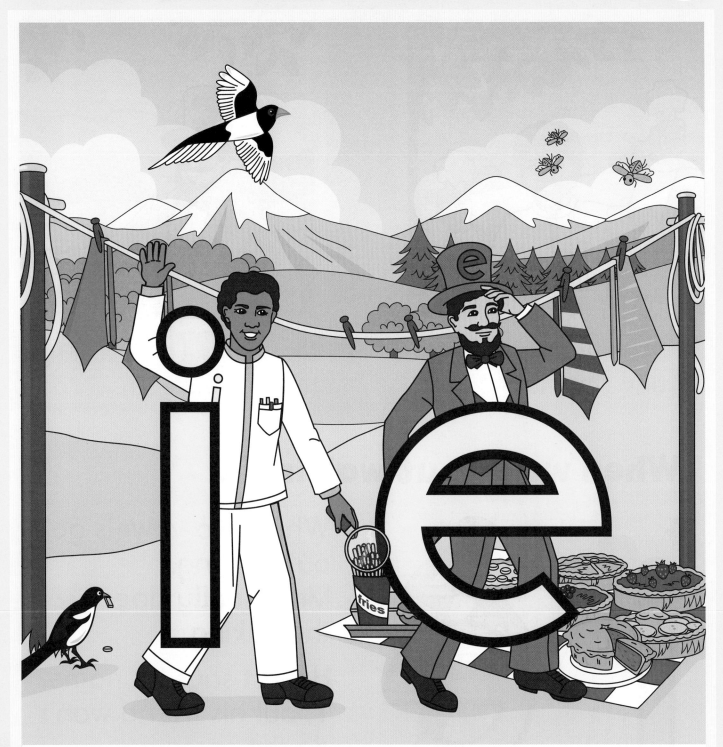

# Mr I and Mr E out walking

**ie digraph**

These are the only Vowel Men who sometimes take turns with the talking (e.g. p**ie** but p**ie**ce, l**ie** but bel**ie**ve).

Find these items in the picture. Listen for Mr I saying his name in the words.

Track 69

pie

tie

flies

fries

magpie

### Phonics Online

Listen to the story about Mr I and Mr E out walking.
Sing along to the song, listen to the sound and play the games.

**Note** Mr E sometimes does the talking in words like: bel**ie**ve, br**ie**f, ch**ie**f, f**ie**ld, n**ie**ce, p**ie**ce, th**ie**f, Ann**ie**.

Workbook When you have finished this page, complete the **ie** activities in *Workbook 1*, pages 55-57.

Workbook

**63**

**Word Building**

Build some **ie** words using *Phonics Online*, or the *Picture Code Cards*.

Code Card

## Build it!

pie, tie, lie, flies.

**Let's read!**

Use the Sound Slide trick to blend the sounds together and read the words. Then try reading the sentences with more fluency.

Let's hide from the flies.

Let's eat pies.

Song

Listen to the Vowels Out Walking song. If you can, join in with the chorus when you listen for the second time.

Track 70

Let's see what happens when Mr I, Golden Girl and Harry Hat Man get together in words.

Hi, I'm Mr I. You know I like to say my name, 'i'.

I'm Golden Girl. I say 'g' in words.

Hello. I'm Harry Hat Man. I whisper 'hhh...' in words.

# When we get together...

When Mr I stands next to Golden Girl he gives her an ice cream for being quiet.

When these three are together, you will only hear Mr I, saying 'i'!

**Letter sounds**

Mr I says '**i**' as he gives Golden Girl an ice cream for being quiet because she knows Harry Hat Man hates noise.

Listen to the story about Mr I, Golden Girl and Harry Hat Man.

Ice cream right →

OPEN AIR THEATRE A KNIGHT'S TALE

## Mr I gives Golden Girl an ice cream

**igh trigraph**

Listen again to the story. This time look for the things in the picture in which you can hear just Mr I saying his name.

Find these items in the picture. Listen for Mr I saying his name in the words.

**light**

**night**

**fight**

**right**

**bright**

### Phonics Online

Listen to the story about Mr I, Golden Girl and Harry Hat Man. Sing along to the song, listen to the sound and play the games.

Workbook When you have finished this page, complete the **igh** activities in *Workbook 1*, pages 58-60.

**67**

Build some **igh** words using *Phonics Online*, or the *Picture Code Cards*.

## Build it!

high, light, night, right.

**Let's read!**

Use the Sound Slide trick to blend the sounds together and read the words. Then try reading the sentences with more fluency.

## The light is on the right.

## We do not like to fight.

**Chant** Listen to the chant. Join in when you listen for the second time. This is a simple practice of **igh** words to a beat.

Track 74

## Story

Let's see what happens when Yellow Yo-yo Man helps out at the end of words.

I'm Yellow Yo-yo Man. I say, 'y'.

I help Mr I at the end of some words.

## Yo-yo Man works for Mr I

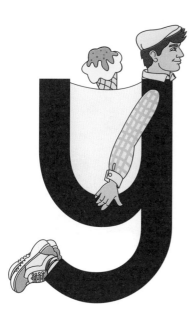

Yellow Yo-yo Man gets a big ice cream from Mr I for taking his place and saying 'I!' for him in words like my, try, and fly.

**Letter sounds** At the end of words, a y can sound like an i.

Look at Yellow Yo-yo Man. Mr I gives him an ice cream whenever he says Mr I's name for him at the end of a word.

# Yellow Yo-yo Man helps Mr I

y as i

Listen to the story and look for the things in which Yellow Yo-yo Man is saying 'i' for Mr I.

Find these items in the big picture.
Listen for Yellow Yo-yo Man saying 'i' for Mr I.

**fly**

**July**

**cry**

**sky**

**why**

### Phonics Online

Listen to the story about Yellow Yo-yo helping Mr I.
Sing along to the song, listen to the sound and play the games.

When you have finished this page, complete the **y as i**
activities in *Workbook 1*, pages 61-63.

Workbook

## Build it!

my, fly, cry, shy.

**Let's read!**

Use the Sound Slide trick to blend the sounds together and read the words. Then try reading the sentences with more fluency.

The bird can fly in the sky.

Why is he crying?

Chant

Listen to the chant. Join in when you listen for the second time. This is a simple practice of **y** words chanted to a beat.

Track 78

Read the stories in *Phonics Readers 4*, featuring the phonic elements in this Unit.

# Comprehension
Point to the correct answer.

**1. How many times does Nick bang the lid on the bin?**

◯ nine ☐ five

**2. Who is on the slide?**

◯ Ben ☐ Mike

**3. What is the name of the teacher?**

◯ Miss Kate ☐ Miss High

**4. What got in Fred's pies?**

◯ five flies ☐ five lies

**5. Who began to cry?**

◯ the duck ☐ the cat

**Pair work**

When you have read the stories, the teacher will read the questions. Work in pairs or small groups to read and point to correct the answers.

**Stickers** ➤ Complete the sticker activity in *Workbook 1*, page 65.

**Listen** ➤ Complete the exercises in *Workbook 1*, pages 66-67.

**Talk time** ➤ This is a first step towards telling the time. Review numbers 1-12. Then, in pairs, ask the time on the three clocks below.

What time is it?

It's five o'clock.

Can you tell me the time, please?

It is six o'clock.

# What time is it?

**Pair work** Look at the clocks and read the times. Practise telling the time whenever you can!

This is Mr E's Magic **e**. The Silent Magic e shoots sparks over one letter to make a Vowel Man appear.

Track 83

## Silent Magic e!

You know this e you cannot hear.

It can make a Vowel Man appear.

hop → hope

not → note

**Letter sounds**    Look how the magic sparks shoot over one letter to make the Vowel Man appear and say his name.

75

Listen to the story about Silent Magic e making Mr O appear.

Track 84

## Magic e makes Mr O appear

o_e split digraph

Listen again to the story. This time look for the things in the picture in which Mr O has appeared to say his name.

**Keywords** ➡

Find these items in the picture. Listen for Mr O saying his name in the words.

Track 85

rose

phone

nose

rope

smoke

### Phonics Online

Listen to the story about Magic **e** making Mr O appear.
Sing along to the song, listen to the sound and play the games.

Letterland Phonics Online

Workbook    When you have finished this page, complete the **o_e** activities in *Workbook 1*, pages 68-70.

Workbook

**77**

## Build it!     hop - hope    not - note

**Let's read!** → Use the Sound Slide trick to blend the sounds together and read the words. Then try reading the sentences with more fluency.

He smells a rose
with his nose.

It is a smoke
free zone.

SMOKE FREE

Song  Listen to the Magic e song. If you can, join in with the chorus when you listen for the second time.

Track
86

Hello. I'm Mr O.
I say my name, 'o'.

Good day. I'm Mr A.
I say my name, 'a'.

# When we go out walking...

When two vowels go out walking, the first one does the talking.

He just says his name, 'o', but his friend won't do the same.

**Letter sounds** The first Vowel Man says his name. The second Vowel Man stays quiet. He's too busy looking out for robots.

Listen to the story about Mr O and Mr A out walking in words.

# Mr O and Mr A out walking

**oa digraph** Listen again to the story. This time look for the things in the picture in which Mr O and Mr A are out walking in the word.

Find these items in the picture. Listen for Mr O saying his name in the words.

Track 89

## boat

## goat

## soap

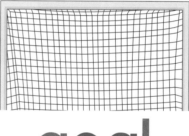

## goal

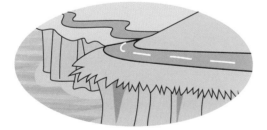

## road

**Phonics Online**

Listen to the story about Mr O and Mr A out walking.
Sing along to the song, listen to the sound and play the games.

Letterland Phonics Online

Workbook — When you have finished this page, complete the **oa** activities in *Workbook 1*, pages 71-73.

Workbook

**81**

Build some **oa** words using *Phonics Online*, or the *Picture Code Cards*.

Code Card

## Build it!

boat, coat, goat
toad, road.

## Let's read!

Use the Sound Slide trick to blend the sounds together and read the words. Then try reading the sentences with more fluency.

# The soap is on the coat.

# The goat is on the road.

 Song

Listen to the Vowels Out Walking song. If you can, join in with the chorus when you listen for the second time.

Track 90

When you see Oscar and Walter together, you can just hear Mr O saying his name. Listen to the reason why.

I'm Oscar Orange.
I say, 'o'.

I'm Walter Walrus.
I say, 'w'.

# Watch out for Walter Walrus!

O...

Walter Walrus teases vowels by splashing them. Mr O is old and he knows a lot, so when he sees Walter he rushes over to Oscar Orange saying, 'Oh no you don't!' Walter is so surprised he makes no sound at all.

**Letter sounds** Watch out when Walter is about! He causes trouble by splashing vowels, but Mr O protects Oscar by stepping in and saying, 'O!'

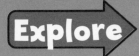 

Listen to the story about Mr O saying **'O!'** to save Oscar Orange from being splashed by Walter Walrus.

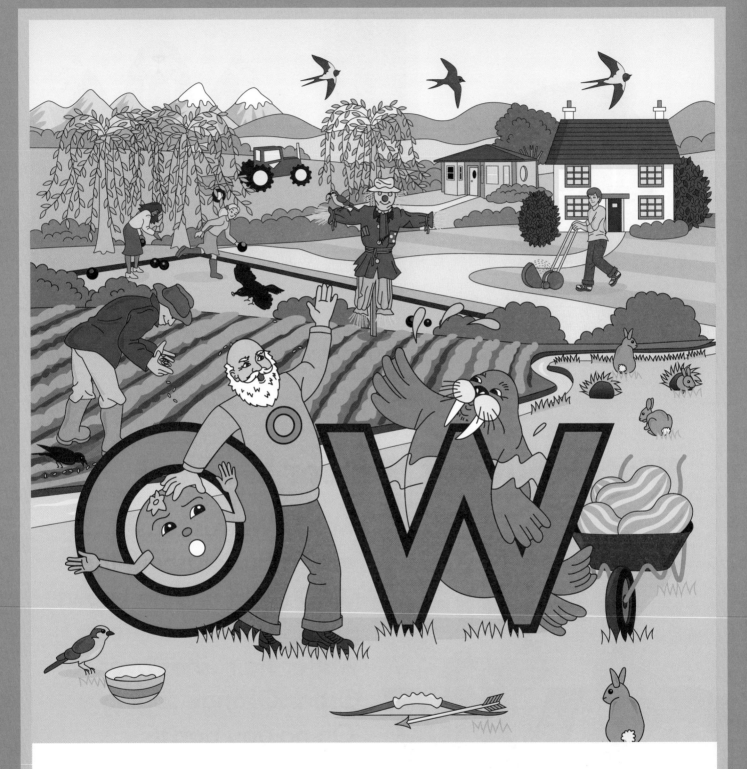

# Mr O and Walter Walrus

 ow digraph

Listen again to the story. This time look for the things in the picture in which Mr O is saying, **'O!'** as he stops Walter from splashing.

Find these items in the picture. Listen for Mr O saying his name in these words.

Track 93

**yellow**

**window**

**snow**

**elbow**

**bowl**

### Phonics Online

Listen to the story about Mr O and Walter Walrus.
Sing along to the song, listen to the sound and play the games.

Betterland Phonics Online

Workbook

When you have finished this page, complete the **ow** activities in *Workbook 1*, pages 74-76.

Workbook

**85**

**Word Building** → Build some **ow** words using *Phonics Online*, or the *Picture Code Cards*.

Code Card

## Build it!

slow, snow,
show, yellow,
window.

**Let's read!** → Use the Sound Slide trick to blend the sounds together and read the words. Then try reading the sentences with more fluency.

The snow is on the window.

This is a big yellow bowl.

86

Chant

Listen to the chant. Then split into two groups. The first group could chant lines 1 & 2, the second group could pretend to be Mr O!

Track 94

Read the stories in *Phonics Readers 5*, featuring the phonic elements in this Unit.

# Comprehension  Point to the correct answer.

**The bad goat**

Focus on: oa as in boat

1. What did Firefighter Fred feed the goat?

◯ **toast**  ☐ **oats**

2. What did Firefighter Fred wash?

◯ **a goat**  ☐ **a foal**

**When the cold wind blows**

Focus on: ow as in snow

3. What do the children do in this story?

◯ **play in snow**  ☐ **play inside**

4. What can you do with the snow?

◯ **cook it**  ☐ **throw it**

**Lost in the Queen's maze**

Focus on: aw as in show

5. Are there arrows to follow in the maze?

◯ **no**  ☐ **yes**

**Pair work**  When you have read the stories, the teacher will read the questions. Work in pairs or small groups to read and point to the correct answers.

**Stickers** → Complete the sticker activity in *Workbook 1*, page 77.

**Listen** → Complete the exercises in *Workbook 1*, pages 79-80.

**Talk time** → In pairs, describe what these people are wearing.
You can use some of the vocabulary below to guide you.

# What is he/she wearing?

He/she is wearing...

a long dress

a long skirt

green trousers

a pink T-shirt

a coat

a hat

a long scarf

a pair of red shoes

a pair of black boots